The Incredible Kids' Craft-IT Series

Transform IT

Written and crafted by Nick Paul and Jack Keely

Illustrated by Jeff Shelly

Transform It Contents

Getting Started

Do you want to learn how to transform plastic bottles into giant bugs? An egg carton into a mummy's tomb? Straw into gold? Well, we can't help you with that last one, but the projects in Transform It can teach you how to turn a pile of trash into a treasure-trove of creative crafts! Starting with some common items like newspapers, jars, boxes—and your imagination—you'll end up with a pile of uncommon crafts that show off your own unique style.

Go over the "Get It" list with a grownup before you start your transformations so you can get some help gathering up your materials. (Sometimes you might need an adult's help with a project too, just to be safe.) In addition to your supplies and your grownup, find some old rags or newspaper to cover your workspace—your parents will appreciate it if you keep things clean!

Most of the supplies you'll need (like tape or cereal boxes) can be found around the house—or rescued from your own trash or recycle bins—but your local art and craft store and grocery market also carry things you might need. Craft glue and decorative hole punches are easy to find at the craft store, and items like corn syrup and plastic wrap are found at almost every market. And if a Transform It activity calls for a special pattern, look to the back of the book, where you'll find a tear-out section of all the patterns you'll need. If you want to make a pattern bigger or smaller to customize your project, ask a grownup to help you duplicate it on a photocopier.

Once you get started, you'll find that the projects in this book are just the beginning of your transforming adventures. It's okay to substitute materials or change the projects to make them unique. When you mix your imagination with the treasures from your trash bin, you're sure to create Transform It projects that are as original as you are!

 Look for this symbol to let you know when a grownup's help is needed.

⚠ Watch It!
Look for this symbol to let you know when special care or precautions are needed.

Make some music with these tuneful toys so everyone will know what's shakin'!

You can transform empty plastic containers into all sorts of faces, monsters, cars, or even houses. Just use tape to create your shape; then cover everything with papier mâché (the newspaper and paste mixture used in step 6). Just be careful if you choose to cover balloons—they can pop and cover you with paste!

Get It!

Lower and upper
  beak patterns (page 33)
Plastic yogurt container with lid
4" x 6" (10 cm x 40 cm)
  heavy cardboard
Cardboard cereal boxes
Small tub wallpaper paste
  (or substitute the "recipe" below)
2 tablespoons dry lentils or beans
Newspaper, cut into 3" (7.5 cm)
  squares
2 plastic bottle caps
Acrylic paints
Medium paintbrush
Clear packing tape
Scissors
Ruler
Stapler

Imagine It!

Instead of using wallpaper paste, try this "recipe":
Mix 3 cups (750 ml) flour and 1 ½ cups (375 ml)
water until the mixture looks like pancake batter.
You've got paste!

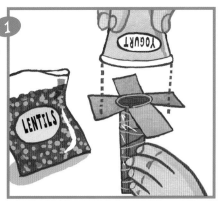

1 Roll the cardboard lengthwise, overlapping it about 1" (2.5 cm), and tape it closed. Cut 4 slits at the top, and bend down the tabs. Put the lentils or beans in the yogurt cup, snap on the lid, and tape the tabs to the top of the upside-down yogurt cup.

2 Cut out the lower beak pattern from a cereal box. Fold it in half, and tape it to the bottom of the yogurt cup to make the lower jaw, letting it stick out about 2" (5 cm). Next stuff the beak with some newspaper to hold its shape.

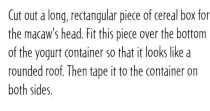

3 Cut out a long, rectangular piece of cereal box for the macaw's head. Fit this piece over the bottom of the yogurt container so that it looks like a rounded roof. Then tape it to the container on both sides.

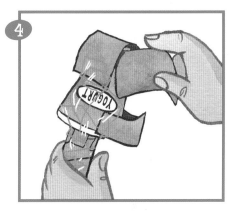

4 Cut out the upper beak pattern from a cereal box. Attach the beak under the "roof," angled down so that it sticks out about 2" (5 cm) beyond the lower beak. Stuff the beak with newspaper; then tape everything together, leaving a mouth opening.

5 Cut out 4 rectangular strips of cereal box. Then cut slits three-quarters of the way down each to make feathers. Tape 2 to the head and 2 to the neck. Then tape on 2 plastic bottle caps to make eyes.

6 Smear paste on the back of a newspaper square and smooth it onto the macaw. Repeat until the maraca is covered completely, and then let it dry overnight. Paint when it's completely dry.

Oatmeal Box Containers

Jungle and sea inspired the daring designs of these flashy, splashy, and fun containers.

It's easy to make this wave-patterned container! Just paint the box and apply crinkled strips of colored tissue paper with water-based glue sealer. Let the container dry and repeat. Then glue on some little plastic balls (like the ones from ponytail holders) to finish!

Get It!

Large and small leaf patterns
 (page 35)
Oatmeal box (or substitute
 other cylindrical box)
Green tissue paper
 (light and dark)
Water-based glue sealer
Cardboard cereal box
White craft glue
Poster paints
Egg carton
Medium or large paintbrush
Scissors

Tropical Plant Container

1 Paint the outside of the oatmeal box green. Then cut 1" (2.5 cm) square pieces of green tissue. When the paint is dry, use glue sealer to cover the box with a layer of dark green tissue squares. Use light green tissue squares to cover the inside.

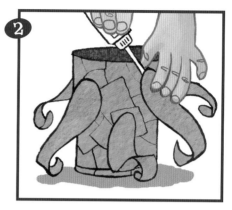

2 Use the large leaf pattern to cut out 4–6 leaf shapes from the cardboard cereal box. Paint them green, and then glue them to the box on top of the layer of green tissue, pointing downward. Space them evenly around the container.

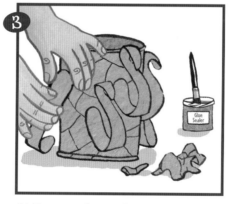

3 Crinkle some small pieces of green tissue to give them texture. Use the sealer to cover the leaves with tissue, one by one. Then add a little more sealer to curve them up. Secure the leaves with craft glue. Then add any additional bits of tissue where needed.

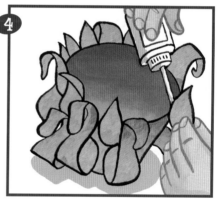

4 Use the small leaf pattern to cut out 4–6 leaf shapes from the cardboard. Then paint them green, and glue them to the top edge of the container, in between the long, curving leaves. Use glue sealer to cover them with tissue. Let them dry.

Imagine It!
It's sometimes easier to work on the lower areas of your container if you turn it upside down. Cut off the top of a two-liter soda bottle just below the shoulder to hold your project while you work on the lower areas.

⚠ Watch It!
This container's great for dried flowers, kitchen utensils, and a whole slew of other dry things, but it's not meant to hold water or other liquids!

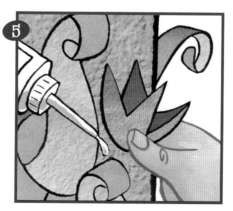

5 Cut several tulip shapes out of the cardboard egg carton, as shown. Paint the flowers, and glue them in between the leaves.

Paper and Plastic Dioramas

Travel through time or to the bottom of the deep blue sea with a 3-D peek into another world.

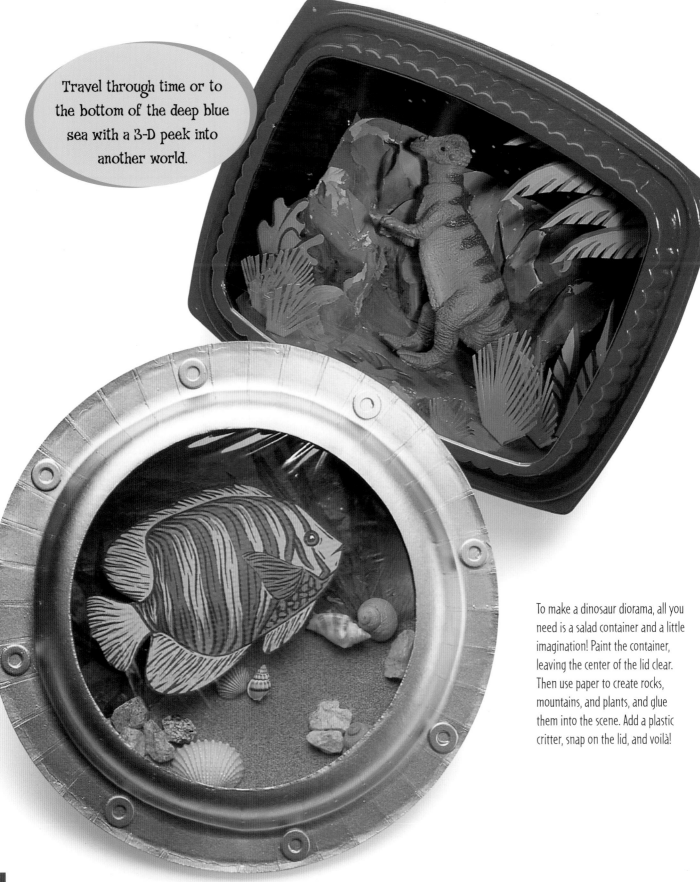

To make a dinosaur diorama, all you need is a salad container and a little imagination! Paint the container, leaving the center of the lid clear. Then use paper to create rocks, mountains, and plants, and glue them into the scene. Add a plastic critter, snap on the lid, and voilà!

Get It!

Fish pattern (page 40)
4 sturdy, deep paper plates
Blue and green tissue paper
Water-based glue sealer
White craft glue
Sandpaper
Shells
Plastic bottle cap
Plastic wrap
Scissors
Small washers
Gold paint
Small paintbrush
Ruler

Porthole Diorama

1 Start by cutting off the outer ½" (1.5 cm) of a plate. Place blue tissue paper over the top two-thirds, and then brush the tissue with glue sealer to make a waterlike background. Create seaweed on top of the blue tissue using green tissue and glue sealer.

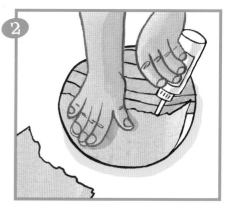

2 Cut out a piece of sandpaper large enough to fill the bottom third of the plate. Use your hands to tear off the top edge of the sandpaper to give it a rough, natural look. Glue the sandpaper to the plate, overlapping the blue and green tissue.

3 Glue a picture of a fish to the center of a new plate, and cut it out. Glue a bottle cap to the center of the decorated plate, and glue the fish to the cap (so it "floats" above the picture).

4 Take a third plate. Cut out the area inside the rim. Cut away the outer ½" (1.5 cm) of the rim. Turn it upside down, cover it with plastic, and glue it to the first plate.

Imagine It!
All types of ordinary boxes can be transformed into decorative dioramas. The deeper the box, the more layers your scene can have!

5 Cut out a circle from the bottom of the fourth plate that is 1" (2.5 cm) from the rim. Glue washers around the outside edge. Paint the plate gold. Let it dry, and then glue it on top of the other plate.

Papier Mâché Box

Bones, claws, and animal patterns decorate a crate ferocious enough to protect the treasures of any wild child!

Where's the coolest place to store your stuff? In ordinary boxes you've transformed with scraps of fabric, fake fur, feathers, popsicle sticks, or any other odds and ends you have!

Get It!

Box with a flap top

Jungle-patterned shopping bag or substitute another fun print

Small tub wallpaper paste, or mix 3 cups (750 ml) flour with 1½ cups (375 ml) water

Brown liquid shoe polish

Medium or large paintbrush

Water-based glue sealer

Paper towels

Newspaper

Two small water bottles

Cardboard cereal box

Scissors

White craft glue

Clear packing tape

Acrylic paint

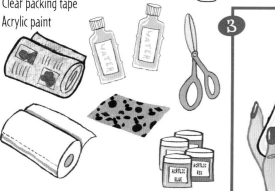

Watch It!

Have a grownup help you cut plastic bottles.

1 Cut the glossy red paper to fit the bottom of the box, and wad it up to give it a crinkled, "alligator skin" look. Stain the creases by painting the bag with watered-down brown shoe polish, then quickly wiping it off with a paper towel.

2 When dry, cut the box flap into a jagged shape. Cover the box with the red paper, as you would wrap a gift. Then crinkle up jungle-patterned wrapping paper, and attach it to the top of the box with glue sealer.

3 To make each foot, ask a grownup to carefully cut a horizontal slit in a water bottle, just above the label, and then cut all the way around the bottle, leaving the cap on. Use water bottles that are big enough to make a steady base for the box.

4 Form claws by cutting out small kite shapes from the cereal box and folding them in half. (Vary the sizes for a wacky effect.) Tape 3 claws to each bottle. Make sure you angle the claws to allow them to balance on a flat surface.

5 Roll up 3 pieces of newspaper, and cut the tubes down to the size you want the bones to be. Then cut the ends of the tubes, and spread them apart to form the bone shape. Wrap them with tape.

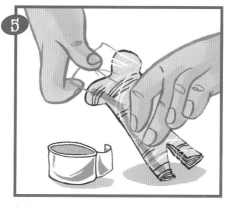

6 Smear paste on newspaper squares, and smooth them over the feet. Cover the feet and bones, and paint them when dry. Glue the feet to the bottom of the box, and glue the bones to the top and sides.

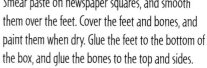

These chic, unique purses are very tasteful—in more ways than one!

These little handbags are perfect for stashing all sorts of important stuff—or keeping snacks close at hand!

Get It!

2 animal-cookie boxes
Self-adhesive contact paper
(or substitute paint)
Pop beads, plastic necklaces, or
beads and twine
Buttons, plastic jewels, leaves, or
other decorations
Fabric fastener circles (like Velcro™)
White craft glue
Scissors

1 Start by cutting off the top and back side of one box, all in one piece. Cut off the edge of the lid that originally tucked inside to close the box. Carefully remove the cloth handle from the other part of the box.

2 Take the piece you removed in step 1, and flip it around backwards; then glue it to the top of the second box. The back of the cut-up box should hang over the front of the whole box. Next round off the end of the flap with scissors.

3 Cover the entire box with contact paper. If you use patterned paper, try to match up the pattern where it meets and overlaps. You may choose to use a solid color of contact paper, or you could even paint the box instead.

4 Push a pencil tip through the slits on the sides of the box to make them a little bigger. Snap pop beads through the slit to make a handle, or use a plastic necklace or twine with beads, gluing the ends down on the inside. Tape the slits shut on the inside.

5 To keep the purse closed, position one part of the fabric fastener on the inside of your purse's flap and the other part on the side of the box.

6 Decorate your handbag with photos of jewels from magazines, or glue on plastic beads or other decorative items.

Bottle Bugs

These creepy, crawly critters came from discarded soda bottles—not the garden!

Water and soda bottles were pieced together with tape to create the friendly bookworm above. Make your own reading buddy by cutting a book, glasses, and "arms" out of a cereal box. We promise he won't "bug" you when you're trying to read your favorite book!

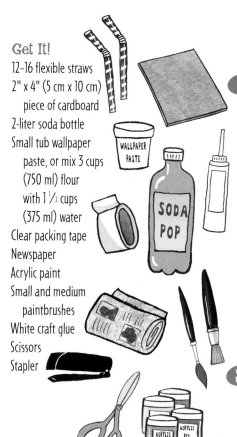

Get It!

12–16 flexible straws

2" x 4" (5 cm x 10 cm) piece of cardboard

2-liter soda bottle

Small tub wallpaper paste, or mix 3 cups (750 ml) flour with 1 1/2 cups (375 ml) water

Clear packing tape

Newspaper

Acrylic paint

Small and medium paintbrushes

White craft glue

Scissors

Stapler

⚠ Watch It!

Have a grownup help cut the plastic bottle—the edges can be sharp.

Bottle Spider

1 Ask a grownup to help you cut off the bottom 2" (5 cm) of the soda bottle. Wad up newspaper and stuff it into the bottle. Tape the paper in the bottle, and turn it upside down to form the spider's body.

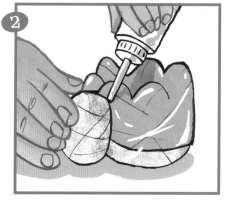

2 Ball up a wad of newspaper to make the spider's head. Make it smooth and round by wrapping the ball with packing tape. Then attach the head to the soda bottle body with craft glue.

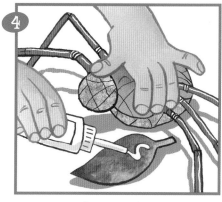

3 Staple 2 flexible straws together at the short ends for legs. (Ours has 6 legs; yours can have 8!) Trim them to the length you want, and tape them to the body.

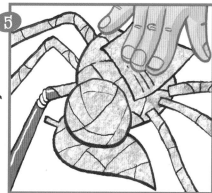

4 Cut the 2" by 4" (5 cm x 10 cm) cardboard into a leaf shape, and glue it under the head so that the spider will balance on a flat surface.

5 Smear wallpaper paste on the back of newspaper squares, and smooth them onto the spider. Cover the spider completely, let it dry overnight, and repeat. Paint the spider when it's completely dry.

Puffy Paper Pillows

Surprise! These pretty, puffy "patchwork" pillows are made from plain old paper bags!

This special pillow lets you hang onto your heart—or hang it anywhere you please! Decorate your pillow with beads and buttons to make it "uniquely you."

Get It!

Puffy pillow patterns
  (pages 37–38)
Paper bags
White craft glue
Poster paint
Twine
Facial tissue
Medium paintbrush
Scissors

Teddy Bear Pillow

Cut out whatever shape you wish to make into a pillow from a brown paper bag (front and back). A simple, large shape works best. Paint your paper shapes with whatever colors or patterns you like. (We used painted stitches to look like patchwork.)

After the paint is thoroughly dry, carefully wad up your creation into a tiny ball. Then flatten it out again, and repeat. As you continue to wad up, flatten, and work the paper with your fingers, it will become softer and more like fabric.

If you want to hang the pillow, make a loop out of twine (add beads if you like), and tie a knot to hold it together. Leave a tail at the end of the knot, and glue the tail to the back panel as shown.

Glue the front of the pillow to the back by placing a thin line of glue around the inside edges of just the top section of the shape. Carefully press the edges together, and then let the glue dry.

Imagine It!
The more you wad up and smooth out your painted design, the softer and more "antique" it becomes.

Stuff the top of the pillow with small bits of facial tissue. When the top is full, glue a few more inches together. Let the glue dry, and continue stuffing and gluing until your pillow is finished.

Egg Carton Creations

Who knew that a fancy mummy's tomb and a mermaid's treasure chest could hatch out of plain old cardboard egg cartons?

Egg cartons come in different shapes and designs. Take a look at the different tops, dividers, and cups the next time you visit the grocery store. You can transform the shapes into flowers, faces, flying saucers, or anything else you can dream up!

Get It!

Mummy's mask pattern with guide (pages 39-40)
2 cardboard (one-dozen) egg cartons
Cardboard cereal boxes
Corrugated cardboard
Old white T-shirt
White craft glue
Poster paint (dark gray, light gray, white, and gold)
Sponge
Small and medium paintbrushes
Scissors

Mummy's Tomb

Take two egg cartons (the type with flat tops and tall, skinny divider pieces between the eggs), and cut the divider pieces out of the center of one carton. Glue the pieces onto the outside of the other carton (in between the egg cups).

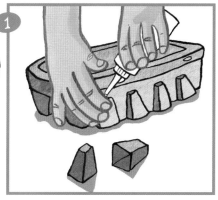

Trace the mummy's mask pattern onto a cereal box panel. Glue this panel to 2 others; then cut out the pattern shapes. Glue the pieces to the lid following the instructions on page 39. Paint some zigzags or other designs on the outside of the case.

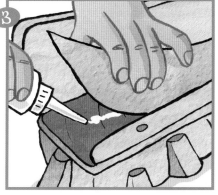

Cut out the tall dividers inside the egg carton, and glue a section from the lid of your second egg carton over the hole. If you have any gaps showing along the sides, cover them with individual rounded pieces of paper.

Paint the inside gold. Then add some black hieroglyphics. Paint the outside dark gray, and then sponge on some lighter grays and whites over the base to look like old stone. With a brush, paint in shadows, and add some details to the face.

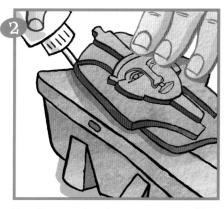

Cut a simple shape from corrugated cardboard for the mummy. Fold in the arms. Add extra layers to make a stomach, chest, brow, and nose. Paint on the eyes.

Cut an old T-shirt into small strips. Wrap them around the mummy until it's covered completely, gluing each strip to the figure.

Get It!

2 cardboard (one-dozen) egg cartons
Cardboard cereal box
Plastic beaded necklace
Newspaper
Scrap paper
Stapler with staples
White craft glue
Poster paint
Clear packing tape
Small and medium paintbrushes
Scissors

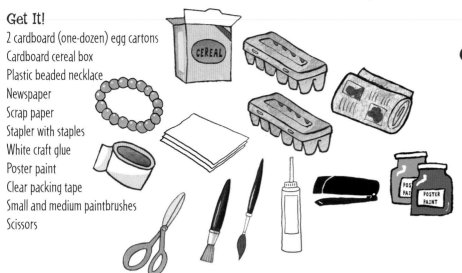

Mermaid's Treasure Chest

1

Use two egg cartons (the kind with a dip in the center of the lid) to start the treasure chest. Cut off the the lid (the whole top half) of the first egg carton. Then glue the top of the first egg carton to the bottom of the second carton.

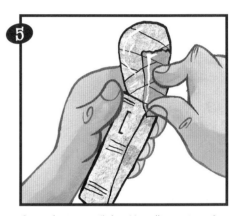

5

Create the mermaid's head by rolling a piece of newspaper into an egg shape. Wrap the head with packing tape so that it holds its shape, and then tape the head to the top of the mermaid's body (from step 4).

9

Glue pieces of yellow-painted cardboard to the head in layers, clipping strands with scissors, and curling them with a pencil.

Glue paper over all four sides of the carton, but don't cover the corner where the cartons begin to curve. Glue a piece of paper at the top of the carton, covering any holes but leaving the dip in the lid for the mermaid to sit on.

Paint the inside and outside of the carton with colors from the sea, such as blue and green. You can draw and paint seashells, starfish, or even sea horses on the box, or you may want to glue on other decorations.

Fold half of one page of newspaper until it's about $\frac{1}{4}$" (6 mm) wide and very thick. Fold this piece in half, leaving about 1" (2.5 cm) of paper sticking out at the top. Staple the newspaper together to form the mermaid's upper body.

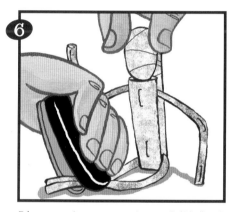

Take a page of newspaper, and cut it in half. Roll both halves into tubes, and tape each tightly. Slip each through the body to make arms and legs. Staple them in place. Then staple the arms to create elbow bends, and staple the legs together at the feet.

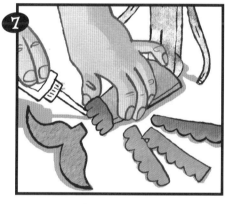

Cut out a fish tail, a cone, and several wavy pieces from a cereal box, paint them, and let them dry. Wrap the cone around the legs, and attach the tail to the ends. Next glue layers of the wavy pieces on top of the cone, starting at the bottom.

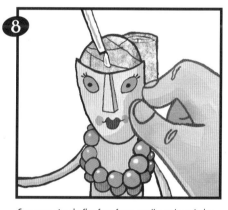

Cut out a simple flat face from cardboard, and glue it to the head. Glue a few small strips of cardboard together to make a nose, and then paint the skin and face. When dry, cut several short strands of the beaded necklace, and glue them to the the chest.

Use a wide piece of cardboard for the bangs and another oval about twice as big for the top of the head. Cut strands; then glue them on top of the head.

Imagine It!

This mermaid can do a lot more than just protect her treasure chest—she can lead a sailing adventure when you create an egg-carton ship! Make a simple boat shape out of egg cartons and a sail out of some extra fabric or an old white T-shirt. Then attach a miniature mermaid figurehead to the front of your ship for protection and luck!

Paper Tube Castle

Your castle can be very small and simple—or towering and complex! Just start with the outer wall, towers, and drawbridge. Then you can create as many wings and additions as you like by using boxes of different shapes and sizes.

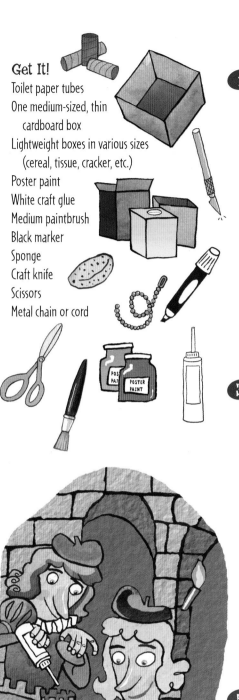

Get It!

Toilet paper tubes
One medium-sized, thin
   cardboard box
Lightweight boxes in various sizes
   (cereal, tissue, cracker, etc.)
Poster paint
White craft glue
Medium paintbrush
Black marker
Sponge
Craft knife
Scissors
Metal chain or cord

1

Start the castle walls with a medium-sized box. Discarded boxes from the grocery or office supply store are good, but it doesn't matter if your castle is square or rectangular. Almost any thin cardboard box of a medium size will work.

3

Cut two long slits on both sides of each corner of the main wall, making sure they're close enough for the tower to slide over the remaining corner. Slide the tower tubes over the corners, and glue them in place.

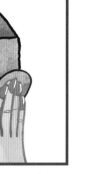

5

Cut matching arches from the front and back of a small box (the gatehouse). Leave the front flap attached at the bottom to form the drawbridge.

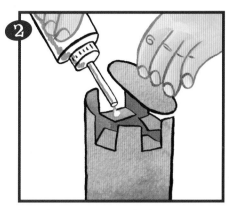

2

Use toilet paper tubes to make the corner towers. Cut evenly spaced tabs along the top of each tube, and then fold in every other tab. Next cut out a circle of cardboard, and glue it on top of the folded tabs to make a roof for the tower.

4

Cut evenly spaced tabs along the wall, and fold every other tab inward. To make a walkway, cut a piece of cardboard the length of the wall. Fold it in half lengthwise. Then glue it to the folded tabs, letting the other side hang down freely.

⚠ **Watch It!**
Have a grownup help with the craft knife.

Paper Tube Castle continued on next page

23

6 Cut tabs along the top of the gatehouse, just as you did on the walls and towers. Then fold every other tab inward. Cut out a rectangular piece of cardboard to fit inside the top of the box, and glue it to the inner tabs as a roof.

7 Cut away a section of the main wall that's a little smaller than the gatehouse. Fold back the extra cardboard on either side of the opening so that the gatehouse fits snuggly, and then glue the gatehouse in place.

8 Now you can glue a few strips of cardboard around the base of the towers if you want to make them look larger. We sponge-painted our basic castle wall, starting with a solid layer of gray, and then adding light gray, lavender, and white.

10 Fold each of the strips in half, with the scored side on the outside. Sponge-paint them with layers of white and gray so that they resemble stone. Let them dry, and then glue them over the corners of the gatehouse.

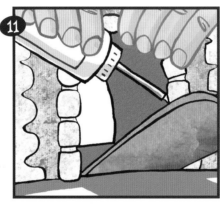

11 Cut out an arched piece of cardboard that's large enough to fit around the drawbridge opening. Cut out waves along the outside edge, and then sponge-paint it to resemble the gatehouse's corners. When dry, glue it over the entryway.

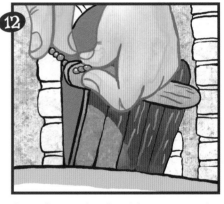

12 Cut out 2 pieces of cardboard the same size and shape as your drawbridge. Paint them to look like wood planks. When dry, glue one to each side of the drawbridge flap. Add a lightweight metal chain or cord to pull up the drawbridge.

14 To add peaked roofs, cut off the top flaps, and then cut a triangle on both sides of the box. Fold in the sides to meet at the peak, and glue together.

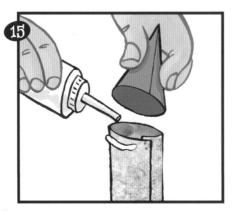

15 Make a set of narrower turrets by rolling up cardboard. Glue each roll closed, and then glue them to the sides of the castle. Add cardboard cones for roofs.

16 Wherever you want to place windows around your castle, draw narrow rectangles, and fill them in with a black marker.

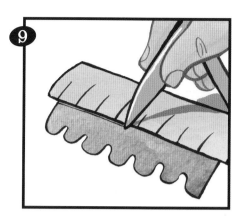

For your gatehouse's corners, cut out four strips of cardboard that are the height of your gatehouse's walls and about 1" (2.5 cm) wide. Cut wavy edges along the sides of the strips, and then score them by running scissors down the middle of the strip.

Create the main part of the castle from five boxes of varying sizes. Add peaked roofs and towers as you did with the castle walls, and then sponge-paint the components. Let everything dry, and then glue the boxes together.

Imagine It!

It's easy to get a stonelike effect with sponge painting. Paint on a solid dark base coat with a brush. Then take a piece of sponge with a lot of holes in it. Mix up a lighter shade of your base color (or a contrasting color), and dip the sponge in it. Blot the sponge a few times to remove extra paint; then begin to gently apply paint to your project. Use as many contrasting shades and layers as you like for a super stone look!

Home Sweet Home never looked so doggone cute as with these picture-perfect photo frames!

FIDO

How can you make your own house? By putting together discarded materials from around your home. Any big box will work for a frame, and tooth-paste boxes make great chimneys. Get creative and decorate your house anyway that you like!

Get It!

3 square, vanity-sized
   tissue boxes
Cardboard cereal box
White craft glue
Poster paint
Medium paintbrush
Scissors

Imagine It!

When gluing together flat areas, such
as shingles or wood trim, use a paper
clip to hold it in place while it dries.

Doghouse

Cut out an arched doorway from the front of one
of the tissue boxes. Then cut out a second arch
from the back, leaving it connected to the box on
one side. Next cut a second tissue box in half diag-
onally, creating a triangular section for the roof.

Cut out pieces from the third tissue box that are
the same size as the doghouse's walls. Glue them
to the sides of the doghouse, with the shiny side
turned in. When dry, paint the doghouse any
color you choose.

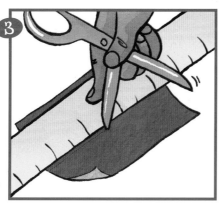

Cut out 4 strips to use as corner pieces; they
should be the height of your doghouse's walls and
$1/2$" (1.5 cm) wide. Score them lightly by running
the blade of your scissors along a ruler placed
down the middle of the strip.

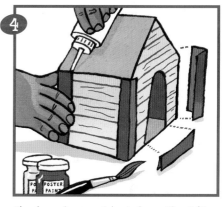

Glue the roof on top of the doghouse. Then fold
the 4 strips in half, with the scored side on the outside. Paint them, let dry, then glue them to the
corners of the doghouse. Repeat to make a step at
the base of the front door and a seam for the roof.

Glue the seam to the roof. Cut out 1" (2.5 cm)
wide cardboard strips a little longer than the roof.
Cut waves in the strips, and glue them to the roof.

Cut a bone shape from a cereal box. Glue squares
of cardboard to the back of the bone. Glue the
bone to the house.

Cut out and create a 3-sided section of tissue box,
as shown. Attach a picture of your dog to the
front, and put it in the doghouse.

Milk Carton Bird Feeders

Leaves, twigs, and twine combine with drink cartons to create a special spot where your feathered friends can dine!

Give the neighborhood birds something to sing about! Add finishing touches like a roof of leaves, additional twigs, or braided twine to make your bird feeder more "homey" before you add seed and hang it from a tree.

Get It!

Milk or juice cartons
Sticks or twigs
Twine
Acrylic paint
Dishwashing liquid
Sandpaper
Medium paintbrush
Craft knife
Scissors
Hole punch

Imagine It!

A hole punch is not only useful, it's also a fun way of decorating a project like this with circular patterns.

⚠ Watch It!

Have a grownup help with the craft knife.

First decide what shape you'd like the opening to be. Measure it out, and draw it on all four sides of the carton. Then have a grownup carefully cut out the four openings with a craft knife.

Lightly sandpaper the container, and then paint it any color you like. (Try adding a drop or two of dishwashing soap to the paint to help it stick to the carton.)

Make a stencil by cutting out an L-shaped piece of paper that's the same size as the corner of your milk carton. Then use a hole punch to make a hole about halfway down from the inside of the "L."

Use the stencil to mark 2 holes below the window of the bird feeder. Then mark these holes in the same place on the opposite side of the feeder. Punch out the 4 holes for your perches.

Push 2 long sticks through the holes on both sides of the feeder. Use twine to tie on small sticks at the front and back of the perches.

Have a grownup poke 2 holes in the top of the container so you can add a handle. Thread a piece of twine through the holes, and tie a knot.

A swirl of confetti and a glimpse of glitter through the glass make these snow domes sparkle and shine.

You can make a snow dome with a single object inside or with two or more glued together. Start by making a simple dome, and then experiment with more elaborate ones!

Get It!

Small, clear jar with
    snug-fitting lid
Small toy or figurine
Corn syrup
Glitter or plastic confetti
Shells, pipe cleaners, or other
    decorations for the base
White craft glue

Pick a jar large enough to hold all the objects you wish to include. Glue the objects to the inside of the jar lid, and allow the glue to dry overnight. Be careful not to glue too closely to the edge, or the jar won't close.

Fill the jar with half water and half corn syrup. The more corn syrup you use, the thicker the solution will be. Stir the mixture together until the corn syrup dissolves. Sprinkle a teaspoon or two of confetti or glitter into the jar.

Screw on the lid tightly, and turn the jar upside down. Dry off the jar, and fill the little area around the cap with a layer of glue to form a water-tight seal.

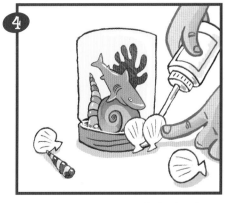

You can give your snow dome a higher base by gluing it on top of another lid. When dry, decorate the base with some fun stuff, such as shells, plastic leaves, ribbons, or pipe cleaners.

Imagine It!

Make a memorable snow dome with trinkets or toys you've collected while on vacation. Your globe will be a unique reminder of your own fun adventures!

Follow-It Project Patterns

This is where you'll find a special tear-out section of all the patterns you'll need. If you want to make a pattern bigger or smaller to customize your project, ask a grownup to help you to enlarge or reduce it on a photocopier.

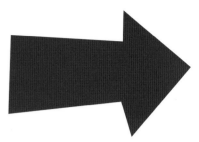

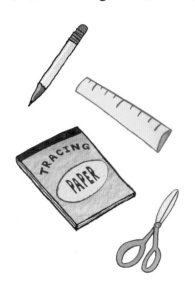

Walter Foster

Walter Foster Publishing, Inc.
23062 La Cadena Drive
Laguna Hills, California 92653
www.walterfoster.com
© 2002 Walter Foster Publishing, Inc.
All rights reserved.

The authors would like to thank George Duckett for providing the porthole diorama craft on pages 8 and 9.
Special thanks to Stephanie Sarracino and the students at Bonita Canyon Elementary School
and to Robyn Allen and the students at Huntington Seacliff Elementary School for their contributions as craft consultants.

Order Code: IT03
ISBN: 1-56010-649-2
UPC: 0-50283-86403-5

Produced by the creative team at Walter Foster Publishing, Inc.:
Sydney Sprague, Associate Publisher
Pauline Foster, Art Director/Designer
Barbara Kimmel, Senior Editor
Samantha Chagollan and Jenna Winterberg, Editors
Carole Thorpe, Production Designer
Toni Gardner, Production Manager
Kathy Beeler, Production Coordinator
Monica Noemi Mijares-DeCuir, Production Artist

Printed in Korea.

Macaw Maraca Beak Patterns (Pages 4-5)

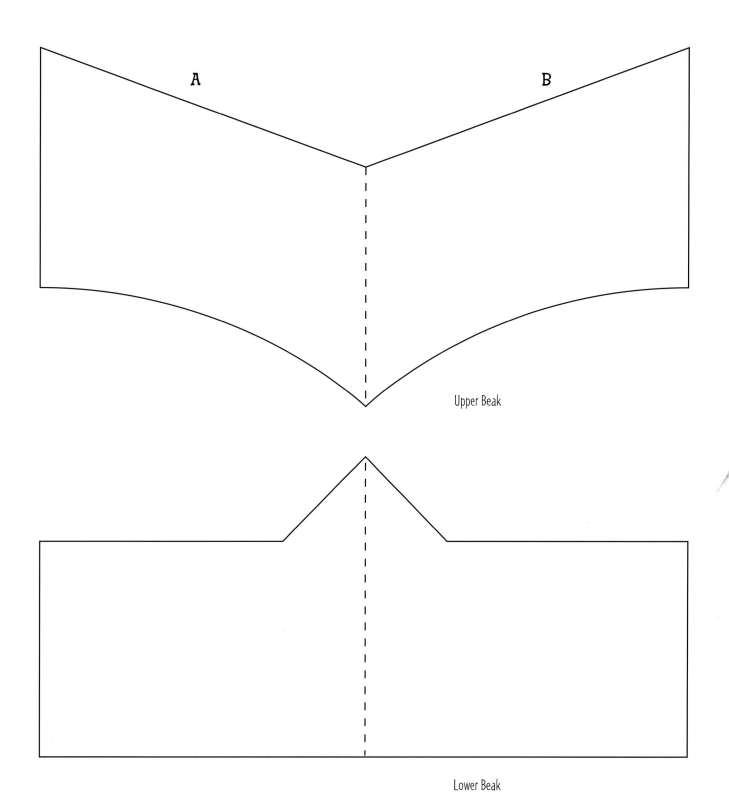

A   B

Upper Beak

Lower Beak

To make the upper beak of the macaw, trace and cut out the pattern above from a cardboard cereal box.
Tape sides A and B together before taping the beak to the macaw.

Oatmeal Box Leaf Patterns (Pages 6-7)

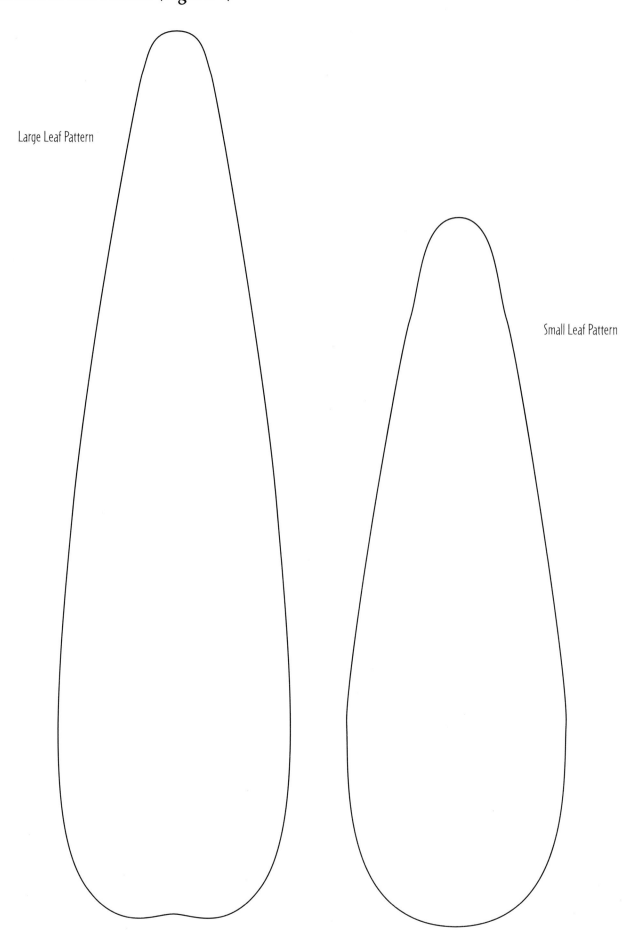

Large Leaf Pattern

Small Leaf Pattern

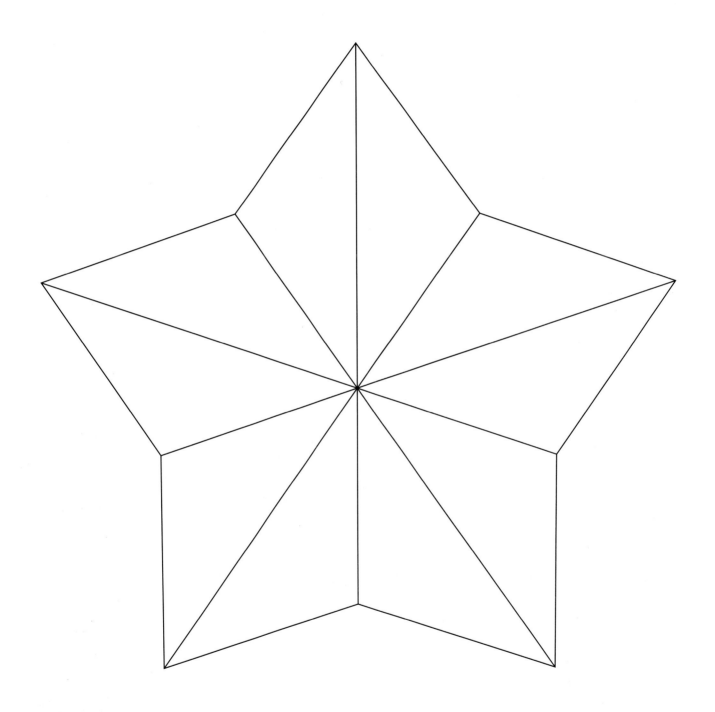

Mummy's Mask Pattern (Page 19)

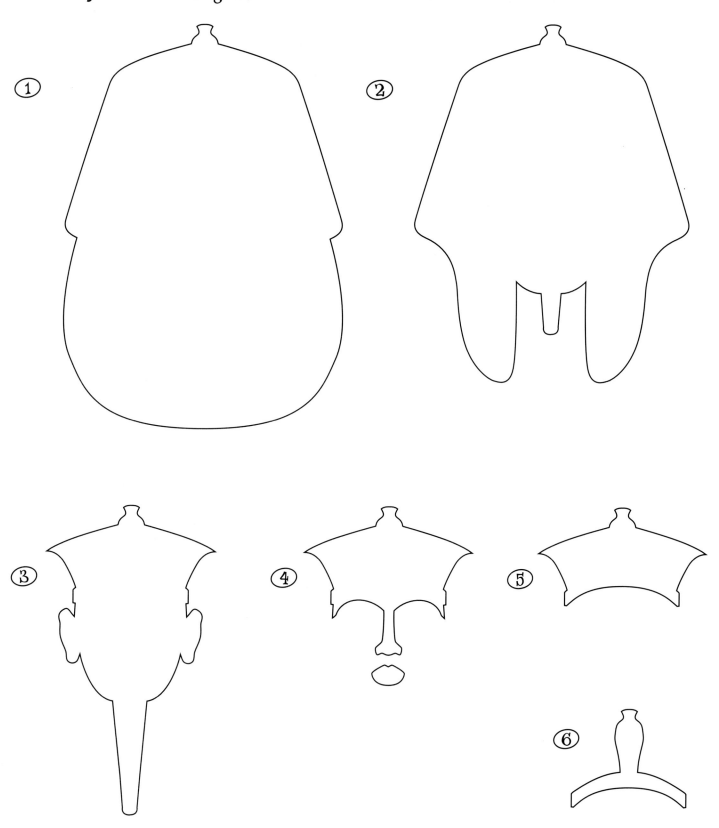

To make the mummy's mask, cut out each of the six pieces from a cereal box or some cardboard. Following the guide on page 40, glue the pieces together in layers. Begin with piece number 1, and add each piece on top of the one before, ending with piece number 6. Then paint on the eyes and eyebrows. When you're finished, your mask should look like the example on page 18.

Fish Pattern (Page 9)

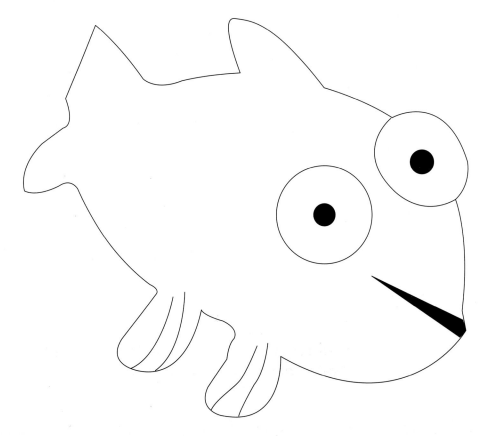